WESTMINSTER S.L.S.

0101154

KT-439-098

Animal Worlds

Animals in the wild

Sue Barraclough

Heinemann
LIBRARY

Little Nippers

WESTMINSTER SCHOOLS LIBRARY SERVICE

www.heinemann.co.uk/library
Visit our website to find out more information about **Heinemann Library** books.

To order:
 Phone 44 (0) 1865 888066
Send a fax to 44 (0) 1865 314091
Visit the Heinemann Bookshop at www.heinemann.co.uk/library to browse our catalogue and order online.

First published in Great Britain by
Heinemann Library, Halley Court, Jordan Hill,
Oxford OX2 8EJ, part of Harcourt Education.
Heinemann is a registered trademark of Harcourt
Education Ltd.

© Harcourt Education Ltd 2006
The moral right of the proprietor has been asserted.

All rights reserved. No part of this publication
may be reproduced, stored in a retrieval system,
or transmitted in any form or by any means,
electronic, mechanical, photocopying, recording,
or otherwise, without either the prior written
permission of the publishers or a licence
permitting restricted copying in the United
Kingdom issued by the Copyright Licensing
Agency Ltd, 90 Tottenham Court Road, London
W1T 4LP (www.cla.co.uk).

Editorial: Sarah Shannon and Dave Harris
Design: Jo Hinton-Malivoire and bigtop design ltd
Picture Research: Ruth Blair and Kay Altwegg
Production: Chloe Bloom

Originated by Modern Age
Printed and bound in China by South China
Printing Company

ISBN 0 431 00364 5 (hardback)
10 09 08 07 06
10 9 8 7 6 5 4 3 2 1

ISBN 0 431 00369 6 (paperback)
10 09 08 07 06
10 9 8 7 6 5 4 3 2 1

British Library Cataloguing in Publication Data
Barraclough, Sue
    Animals in the wild. - (Animal worlds)
    590
A full catalogue record for this book is available
from the British Library.

Acknowledgements
The publishers would like to thank the following
for permission to reproduce photographs:
Corbis pp. 9, 18, 19; FLPA p. 17; FLPA/David
Hosking p. 13; FLPA/Frans Lanting/Minden
Pictures pp. 10, 16; FLPA/Frits Van Daalen/Foto
Natura p. 6; FLPA/Gerard Lacz p. 17, 19;
FLPA/Hannu Hautala p. 11; FLPA/Michio
Hoshino/Minden Pictures p. 20; FLPA/Panda
Photo p. 7; FLPA/Terry Whittaker p. 23; FLPA/Yva
Momatiuk & John Eastcott/Minden Pictures p. 12;
Getty Images/Digital Vision p. 14; NHPA/Jonathan
& Angela Scott p. 22; NHPA/Melvin Grey p. 21;
NHPA/Michael Leach p. 8; OSF pp. 4, 5.

Cover photograph reproduced with permission
of photolibrary.com/osf.

Every effort has been made to contact copyright
holders of any material reproduced in this book.
Any omissions will be rectified in subsequent
printings if notice is given to the publishers.

The paper used to print this book comes from
sustainable resources.

Contents

There are lots of different wild animals.

4

Wild animals have to find food and water. These animals have come for a drink.

This elephant drinks water through its trunk.

5

Different wild animals

Wild animals come in all shapes and sizes.

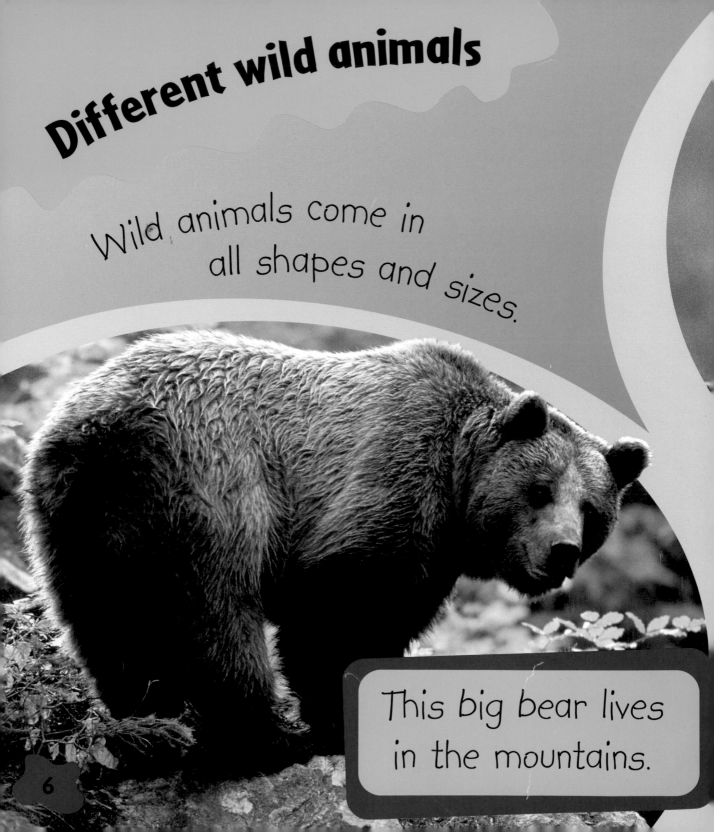

This big bear lives in the mountains.

Squirrels live in many different places.

Do you know what squirrels like to eat?

Nests and burrows

Some wild animals make their homes under the ground.

Rabbits live in homes called burrows.

This animal is called a raccoon. It makes its nest high up in a tree.

MUNCH

MUNCH

Wild animals need food to stay healthy.

Giraffes have long necks to reach leaves high in the trees.

All animals need water to drink. This bird drinks from a pool.

Animals in the air

Some animals have wings and can fly.

Bats fly around at night.

Many birds fly in big groups called flocks.

What do you think these gulls are looking for?

Animals in the water

Some wild animals live underwater.

These fish live in the ocean. They swim around the coral to look for food.

Moving around

Kangaroos have strong back legs for hopping along.

BOING!

Orangutans have long arms . for swinging through trees.

Dolphins use their tails to push them through the water.

Making noises

Wild animals make
all kinds of noises.

Wolves howl.

ow-ow-OWWW!

Tigers growl.

GRRRRR!

Can you squawk like a parrot?

SQUAWK!

Baby wild animals

Animals take care of their babies.

These polar bear cubs stay close to their mother.

Birds find food for their young.

This bird caught a caterpillar
for her babies to eat.

Caring and cleaning

Wild animals take good care of each other.

Lions use their tongues to lick their fur clean.

Baboons use their fingers to clean each other.

23

Index

Notes for adults

This series supports a young child's knowledge and understanding of their world. The following Early Learning Goals are relevant to the series:

• Find out about, and identify, some features of living things, objects, and events that they observe.

• Develop communication, language and literacy by imitating different animal sounds, and to notice and describe similarities and differences.

These books will help children extend their vocabulary, as they will hear some new words. Since words are used in context in the book this should enable young children to gradually incorporate them into their own vocabulary.

This series investigates a variety of animals by looking at distinguishing features and characteristics and by exploring their different environments.

Follow-up activities:

Encourage children to think about any wild animals they have seen in parks and gardens, and to draw a picture of their favourite animal and where it lives.